I0803364

What Is Biblical Church Leadership?

9Marks Healthy Church Study Guides

Built upon the Rock: The Church

Hearing God's Word: Expositional Preaching

The Whole Truth about God: Biblical Theology

God's Good News: The Gospel

Real Change: Conversion

Reaching the Lost: Evangelism

Committing to One Another: Church Membership

Guarding One Another: Church Discipline

Growing One Another: Discipleship in the Church

Leading One Another: Church Leadership

Talking to God: Prayer

Sending and Going Together: Missions

What Is Biblical Church Leadership?

Small Group Study Guide

Bobby Jamieson

Mark Dever, General Editor

Jonathan Leeman, Managing Editor

IX 9Marks

CROSSWAY®

WHEATON, ILLINOIS

What Is Biblical Church Leadership?: Small Group Study Guide

© 2025 by 9Marks

Published by Crossway
1300 Crescent Street
Wheaton, Illinois 60187

All rights reserved. No part of this publication may be reproduced, stored in a retrieval system, or transmitted in any form by any means, electronic, mechanical, photocopy, recording, or otherwise, without the prior permission of the publisher, except as provided for by USA copyright law. Crossway® is a registered trademark in the United States of America.

This study guide is adapted from Bobby Jamieson, *Leading One Another: Church Leadership* (Wheaton, IL: Crossway, 2012). Used by permission.

Cover design: Jordan Singer

Cover image: Getty Images

First printing 2025

Printed in China

Unless otherwise indicated, Scripture quotations are from the ESV® Bible (The Holy Bible, English Standard Version®), © 2001 by Crossway, a publishing ministry of Good News Publishers. Used by permission. All rights reserved. The ESV text may not be quoted in any publication made available to the public by a Creative Commons license. The ESV may not be translated in whole or in part into any other language.

Scripture quotations marked NIV are taken from the Holy Bible, New International Version®, NIV®. Copyright © 1973, 1978, 1984, 2011 by Biblica, Inc.™ Used by permission of Zondervan. All rights reserved worldwide. www.zondervan.com. The "NIV" and "New International Version" are trademarks registered in the United States Patent and Trademark Office by Biblica, Inc.™

Trade paperback ISBN: 978-1-4335-7961-5

Crossway is a publishing ministry of Good News Publishers.

RRD 34 33 32 31 30 29 28 27 26 25
15 14 13 12 11 10 9 8 7 6 5 4 3 2 1

Contents

How to Use This Book

This study guide aims to help congregations understand God's design for church leadership and gladly embrace it. It consists of six lessons and can be used in a wide variety of contexts: Sunday school classes, small groups, retreats, committee meetings, and more. The context and pace can be adapted for your unique circumstances.

You'll notice that this study guide does not include lengthy readings or exposition. Instead, it's designed to get participants interacting with the text of Scripture so that they inductively discover a biblical pattern for church leadership. Teachers of this guide should remember to encourage participants to answer questions in light of the Scripture passages listed in the current lesson. At the end of this guide is a section of Teacher's Notes with answers to the discussion questions, which will help leaders teach through the guide in a group. This study guide also contains URLs for six audio interviews that correspond to the six lessons. These audio interviews are designed to provide additional pastoral instruction. Overall, we hope this guide serves congregations as they endeavor to implement biblical leadership.

Introduction

Audio link: *https://www.9marks.org/church-leadership-introduction/*

What does the local church mean to you?

Maybe you love your church. You love the people. You love the preaching, the singing. You can't wait to show up on Sunday, and you cherish fellowship with other church members throughout the week.

Maybe the church is just a place you show up to a couple times a month. You sneak in late, duck out early.

In the Bible, the local church is God's plan for displaying his glory to the nations. And we want to help you catch and live out that vision, together with your whole church.

This guide includes six lessons on biblical leadership. Each lesson takes a close look at one or more passages of Scripture and considers how it applies to the life of the whole church.

These studies are mainly driven by observation, interpretation, and application questions, so get ready to speak up! We also hope that these studies provide opportunities for believers to reflect together on their experiences in the church, whatever those experiences may be.

Leaders can make life much better or much worse, can't they? Think of loving parents who make countless sacrifices for their children's good, a gifted teacher who not only instructs but also inspires, a wise head of state who pursues justice and peace, or a pastor who faithfully teaches, preaches, counsels, and cares for his people. On the other hand, we are all too familiar with abusive or irresponsible parents, teachers who are lazy or uncaring, oppressive military dictators, and pastors who spout heresy and fleece their flocks.

In light of the good and the bad you've likely seen in the church, we need to go back to the Bible to understand what a church is and how God intends for it to be led. In the first lesson of this study, we'll consider what it means for Christ to be the head of the church and whether Scripture is sufficient to govern the church. The second lesson answers the question, Is authority bad? It also explores the nature of good authority and God's design for how it should function in the church. The remaining lessons in the study consider individuals who have special responsibilities within the church: elders, deacons, and members (like you!).

Because it can be abused, leadership is a risky business for those in it and those under it. But God has good plans for leadership within the church. Let's explore those plans together and ask him to bless our churches with leaders—shepherds, in fact—after his own heart.

An Important Mark of a Healthy Church: Biblical Church Leadership

By Mark Dever

Adapted from *What Is a Healthy Church?*

What kind of leadership does a healthy church have? Is it a congregation that strives to ensure that the gospel is faithfully preached? Yes (Gal. 1). Is it deacons who model service in the affairs of the church? Yes (Acts 6). Is it a pastor who is faithful in preaching the word of God? Yes (2 Tim. 4). But the Bible presents one more leadership gift to churches to help them become healthy: the position of elder.

Surely there are many useful things we could say about church leadership from the Bible; yet I want to focus primarily on this question of elders, since I fear a lot of churches don't know what they're missing. As a pastor, I pray that Christ will place within our fellowships men whose spiritual gifts and pastoral concern indicate that God has called them to be elders. May he prepare many such men! If God has so gifted a certain man in the church with exemplary character, pastoral wisdom, and gifts of teaching, and if, after prayer, the church recognizes these things, then he should be set apart as an elder.

WHAT IS AN ELDER?

In Acts 6, the young church in Jerusalem began to bicker over how food was being distributed to widows. The apostles therefore called upon the church to select several men who could better oversee this distribution. The apostles chose to delegate this particular task so that they could then "give [their] attention to prayer and the ministry of the word" (Acts 6:4 NIV).

That, in the briefest terms, appears to be the division of labor between elders and deacons that the rest of the New Testament develops. Elders are especially devoted to prayer and the ministry of the word for the church, while deacons help sustain the church's physical operations.

Are you beginning to see what a gift this is to you, churches? God is essentially saying that he is going to take several men from among you and set them aside to pray for you and teach you about him.

ELDERS AND CONGREGATIONS

All churches have had individuals designated to perform the functions of elders, even if those individuals are called by other titles, such as "deacon" or "director." The three New Testament titles for this office, which are used interchangeably, are *episkopos* (overseer or bishop), *presbuteros* (elder), and *poimain* (shepherd or pastor). All three are used for the same men, for instance, in Acts 20:17 and 20:28.

When evangelicals hear the word "elder," however, many of them immediately think "Presbyterian." Yet the first Congregationalists (capital *C*, pointing to a formal group of churches) back in the sixteenth century taught that eldership was an office for New Testament churches. Elders could also be found in Baptist churches in America throughout the eighteenth and into the nineteenth centuries. In fact, the first president of the Southern Baptist Convention, W. B. Johnson, wrote a treatise in 1846 calling Baptist churches to use a plurality of elders, arguing that the practice was biblical.

Baptists and Presbyterians do disagree in two areas concerning elders (and I think the issues at play here are relevant to those who are not Baptist or Presbyterian). First and most fundamentally, we who are Baptists are congregationalists (lowercase *c*, referring to a practice). We believe that the Bible teaches that the final decision on matters rests with the congregation as a whole, not with a church's elders or anyone outside the church body. When Jesus was teaching his disciples about confronting a sinful brother, he said that the congregation was the final court of appeal—not the elders, not a bishop or pope, not a council or convention (Matt. 18:17). When the apostles sought out several men to act as deacons, as we just discussed, they gave the decision over to the congregation.

In Paul's letters, too, the congregation appears to assume final responsibility. In 1 Corinthians 5, he blames not the pastor, elders, or deacons for tolerating a man's sin but the congregation. In 2 Corinthians 2, Paul refers to what a majority of them had done in disciplining an erring member. In Galatians 1, he calls on the congregations themselves to judge the false teaching they had been hearing. In 2 Timothy 4, he reproves not just the false teachers but also those who paid them to teach what their itching ears wanted to hear. Thus, elders lead, but they do so, biblically and necessarily, within the bounds recognized by the congregation. In that sense, elders and every other board or committee in a Baptist church act in what is finally an advisory capacity to the whole congregation.

Second, Baptists and Presbyterians have disagreed over the roles and responsibilities of elders, largely due to different understandings of the following words written by Paul for Timothy: "The elders who direct the affairs of the church well are worthy of double honor, especially those whose work is preaching and teaching" (1 Tim. 5:17 NIV). Presbyterians understand this verse as establishing two classes of elders—ruling elders and teaching elders. Baptists don't recognize this formal division but understand the verse to suggest that certain individuals among a group of elders will simply be given more fully, as a practical matter, to preaching and teaching. After all, Paul clearly tells Timothy earlier in the letter that a basic qualification of every elder is that he is "able to teach" (1 Tim. 3:2; see Titus 1:9). Baptists, therefore, have often denied the appropriateness of appointing elders who are not capable of teaching Scripture.

A PLURALITY OF ELDERS

What Baptists and Presbyterians often agreed on in the eighteenth century was that there should be a plurality (or multiple number) of elders in each local church. The New Testament never suggests a specific number of elders for a particular congregation, but it clearly and consistently refers to the "elders" of a local church in the plural (e.g., Acts 14:23; 16:4; 20:17; 21:18; Titus 1:5; James 5:14). Today, not only are more and more Baptist churches rediscovering this but also churches from many other denominations as well as independent churches.

A plurality of elders does not mean that the pastor has no distinctive role. There are many references in the New Testament to preaching and preachers that would not apply to all the elders in a congregation. In Corinth, for instance, Paul gave himself exclusively to preaching in a way that lay elders in a church could not (Acts 18:5; 1 Cor. 9:14; 1 Tim. 4:13; 5:17). Also, preachers seemed to relocate to an area for the express purpose of preaching (Rom. 10:14–15), whereas elders seemed settled among the community (Titus 1:5).

As the regular voice that proclaims God's word, a faithful preacher will probably find that a congregation and the other elders treat him as the first among equals and "especially" worthy of double honor (1 Tim. 5:17). Still, the preacher or pastor is, fundamentally, just one more elder, formally equal with every other man called by the congregation to act in this capacity.

THE BENEFITS OF ELDERS

My own experience as a pastor has confirmed the usefulness of following the New Testament practice of sharing, wherever possible, the responsibility for pastoring a local church with other men rooted in the congregation.

Decisions involving the church but not requiring the attention of all the members should fall not to the pastor alone but to the elders as a whole. This is sometimes cumbersome, but it has immense benefits. It rounds out the pastor's gifts, making up for some of his defects and supplementing his judgment. It creates support in the congregation for decisions, helping unity and leaving leaders less exposed to unjust criticism. It makes leadership more rooted and permanent and allows for more mature continuity. It encourages the church to take more responsibility for its spirituality and helps make the church less dependent on its employees.

This practice of a plurality of elders is unusual among Baptist churches today, but there is a growing trend toward it among Baptists and many others—and for good reason. It was needed in New Testament churches and it is needed now.

WHAT ABOUT DEACONS?

Unfortunately, many modern churches also tend to confuse elders with either the church staff or the deacons. Deacons also fill a New Testament office, one rooted in Acts 6, as we saw. While any absolute distinction between the two offices is difficult, deacons are generally concerned with the practical details of church life: administration, maintenance, and the care of church members with physical needs. In many churches today, the deacons have either taken over the role of spiritual oversight or they have left it entirely in the hands of one man, the pastor. But it would benefit churches to again distinguish the roles of elders and deacons. Do churches not need both types of servants?

SHOULDERING THE BURDEN AND PRIVILEGE

Eldership is the biblical office that I hold as a pastor—I am the main preaching elder. But I work together with a group of elders for the edification of the church. Some are on staff, but the majority are not. We meet regularly to pray, to talk, and to form recommendations for the deacons or the whole church. It's difficult to put into words how much these men have loved both me and our entire congregation by sharing the burden—and privilege—of pastoring. I thank God regularly for these fellow workers.

Clearly, eldership is a biblical idea that has practical value. If implemented in our churches, it could help pastors immensely by removing weight from their shoulders and even removing their own petty tyrannies from their churches. Furthermore, the character qualities listed by Paul for eldership, aside from the ability to teach, are qualities every Christian should work toward (1 Tim. 3; Titus 1). Publicly affirming certain individuals as exemplary, then, helps to present a model for other Christians, especially Christian men. Indeed, the practice of recognizing godly, discerning, trusted laymen as elders is another mark of a healthy church.

LESSON 1

Who Runs the Church?

Audio link: *https://www.9marks.org/church-leadership-lesson-1/*

GETTING STARTED

1. What are some of the different ways you've seen church leadership structured? What were pros and cons of those different leadership models?

2. Do you think the Bible gives instructions about how to structure church leadership? If so, what are they? What are some ways you think your local church could do a better job of obeying the Bible's instructions on this issue?

Visit a dozen churches and you might find a dozen different ways that they organize their leadership. So who's right? Even more, how would we know who's right? This lesson explores answers to these questions by reminding us that the church doesn't belong to us but to Jesus. And his word is sufficient to govern the life and structure of the church.

MAIN IDEA

Christ is king over the church so his word must govern the church, including its leadership structures.

DIGGING IN

In Ephesians 5, the apostle Paul teaches the Ephesian church about marriage and the obligations God has for husbands and wives. But all of Paul's teaching on marriage is rooted in his understanding of how Christ relates to the church. Verses 22–27 say,

> [22] Wives, submit to your own husbands, as to the Lord. [23] For the husband is the head of the wife even as Christ is the head of the church, his body, and is himself its Savior. [24] Now as the church submits to Christ, so also wives should submit in everything to their husbands. [25] Husbands, love your wives, as Christ loved the church and gave himself up for her, [26] that he might sanctify her, having cleansed her by the washing of water with the word, [27] so that he might present the church to himself in splendor, without spot or wrinkle or any such thing, that she might be holy and without blemish.

1. How does Ephesians describe Christ's relationship to the church?

2. What does it mean for Christ to be the "head" of the church?

3. How is the church supposed to respond to Christ's headship?

Christ is the head of the church, and we therefore submit everything in the church to his wise and gracious reign. He orders the church. That means Scripture, the word of King Jesus, must govern the church's life and structure. Yet Scripture is not only the *authoritative* word of King Jesus but also a *sufficient* word: "All Scripture is breathed out by God and profitable for teaching, for reproof, for correction, and for training in righteousness, that the man of God may be complete, equipped for every good work" (2 Tim. 3:16).

4. What does it mean that Scripture is "breathed out by God"? What implication does this have for the authority of Scripture?

5. Scripture equips us for "every good work" (2 Tim. 3:17). What does this phrase tell us about the sufficiency of Scripture?

6. What are the implications of the sufficiency of Scripture for how a church organizes its leadership?

Paul was a church planter. And he cared about how those churches were ordered and the leadership structures they used. He wanted them to follow the commands of King Jesus—the head of the church. One place in Scripture that makes this point is Titus 1:5. Here, Paul said to his protégé Titus, "This is why I left you in Crete, so that you might put what remained into order, and appoint elders in every town as I directed you."

7. What do you think Paul means by commanding Timothy to put the church "into order"? What are some implications of the fact that Paul uses the word "order" in this passage?

8. What is the first thing Paul tells Timothy to do to start getting the church "in order"?

In Titus 1:5, Paul shows that biblical church order requires biblical church leadership when he commands Titus to "appoint elders." The rest of this study guide will examine biblical leadership in detail. For now, let's focus on the big picture. Read these passages on leadership in the church: Acts 6:1–7, Acts 20:17–38, 1 Timothy 3, and 1 Peter 5:1–5.

9. According to these scriptures, how many leadership offices exist in the church and what are they?

10. According to these scriptures, what are the differences between elders and deacons?

11. In your opinion, why are some churches not willing to follow the Bible's blueprint for church leadership?

12. What are some ramifications of not following the Bible's teaching on church leadership?

13. What are some experiences you've had with churches that followed Scripture's teachings on biblical leadership? What are some experiences you've had with churches that didn't follow these instructions? How did that positively or negatively affect that church?

LESSON 2

Is Authority Bad?

Audio link: *https://www.9marks.org/church-leadership-lesson-2/*

GETTING STARTED

1. What kind of authority relationships are you in? Whose authority are you under? Do you exercise authority over anyone?

2. What are some experiences with authority you've had that stand out to you? Were they good, bad, or ugly?

Before we get into the weeds on what the Bible says about church leadership, we need to talk about an even bigger issue: authority. Many in our culture are highly suspicious of authority—after all, it can be used to oppress, abuse, and denigrate people. The fact that authority is so often abused has led some people to regard it as inherently evil itself. But, as we'll see from Scripture, authority is from God, for our good, and images his righteous ruling of the universe.

MAIN IDEA

Authority is a good gift from God that images his rule over us.

DIGGING IN

In Daniel 4, God sends Nebuchadnezzar, the king of Babylon, out into the wilderness. God throws him down from his high place and causes him to live as a wild beast so that he would learn who rules the universe. At the end of this episode, Nebuchadnezzar says,

> 34 I, Nebuchadnezzar, lifted my eyes to heaven, and my reason returned to me, and I blessed the Most High, and praised and honored him who lives forever,

for his dominion is an everlasting dominion,
    and his kingdom endures from generation to generation;
35 all the inhabitants of the earth are accounted as nothing,
    and he does according to his will among the host of heaven
    and among the inhabitants of the earth;
and none can stay his hand
    or say to him, "What have you done?" (Dan. 4:34–35)

1. What does Nebuchadnezzar say about God's relationship to humanity? How would you describe that relationship?

____

____

____

____

____

____

2. How does your heart react to idea that God rules over everything and does all that he pleases in heaven and on earth?

____

____

____

____

____

In Genesis 1, we read that God created the whole universe, including the earth and humankind. When he created humans, he said,

> [26] "Let us make man in our image, after our likeness. And let them have dominion over the fish of the sea and over the birds of the heavens and over the livestock and over all the earth and over every creeping thing that creeps on the earth."
>
> [27] So God created man in his own image,
> in the image of God he created him;
> male and female he created them.
>
> [28] And God blessed them. And God said to them, "Be fruitful and multiply and fill the earth and subdue it and have dominion over the fish of the sea and over the birds of the heavens and over every living thing that moves on the earth." (Gen. 1:26–28)

3. What does being made in the image of God mean for humanity's relationship to creation (Gen. 1:26, 28)?

4. What do we learn about authority from this passage?

King David had more experience with authority than most people in the Bible. He knew what good came when authority was used wisely, and he knew by sad experience what happened when people abused authority—because he did so himself (2 Sam. 11–12). It should arrest our attention, then, that David's last words, which are recorded for us in 2 Samuel 23, are about authority. Verses 1–4 read,

1 The oracle of David, the son of Jesse,
the oracle of the man who was raised on high,
the anointed of the God of Jacob,
the sweet psalmist of Israel:
2 "The Spirit of the Lord speaks by me;
his word is on my tongue.
3 The God of Israel has spoken;
the Rock of Israel has said to me:
When one rules justly over men,
ruling in the fear of God,
4 he dawns on them like the morning light,
like the sun shining forth on a cloudless morning,
like rain that makes grass to sprout from the earth."

5. According to David, what happens when a king rules justly and in the fear of God? Have you ever experienced fruit like this in your own life from the godly exercise of authority?

6. In light of all of these passages, how would you respond to someone who thought that authority itself was a bad thing?

So what does good authority look like? To answer this question we need to look at how God exercises authority. As we do, we'll discover some important truths about his design for authority in the church.

One place we learn about good and bad authority is Ezekiel 34. It is a sweeping passage. In it, God condemns the wickedness of the shepherds of Israel, reveals his own character as the shepherd of his people, and promises to deliver his people in the future.

7. Read Ezekiel 34:1–24. What have the shepherds of Israel done? What have they not done (vv. 1–4)? What are some of the concrete events that this metaphorical language is probably referring to (vv. 18–19)?

8. What has happened to the people of Israel as a result of the shepherd's unrighteousness and negligence (vv. 5–6)?

9. What are all the different things God promises to do for his sheep (vv. 11–16)? List them.

10. What do God's promises in verses 11–16 reveal about his character and the nature of good authority?

11. Who does God promise to set up over his flock after he rescues them (vv. 22–24)?

12. How does God fulfill this promise (see Jer. 23:5–6; Luke 1:32–33; John 10:11–18)?

13. In Jeremiah 3:14, God promises to gather his people to Israel again, just as he promised in Ezekiel 34. But then in Jeremiah 3:15 we see another facet of God's redemptive plan. He says, "I will give you shepherds after my own heart, who will feed you with knowledge and understanding." What does this prophecy add to our understanding of how God will shepherd his people? How is this prophecy fulfilled? (See Eph. 4:8–12.)

You may be surprised to learn that the word our English Bibles render "pastor" actually means "shepherd" in Greek. Thus when we read about pastors in the Bible, we should think about shepherds. That's why Peter writes to the elders of local churches,

> [1] I exhort the elders among you, as a fellow elder and a witness of the sufferings of Christ, as well as a partaker in the glory that is going to be revealed: [2] shepherd the flock of God that is among you, exercising oversight, not under compulsion, but willingly, as God would have you; not for shameful gain, but eagerly; [3] not domineering over those in your charge, but being examples to the flock. [4] And when the chief Shepherd appears, you will receive the unfading crown of glory. (1 Pet. 5:1–4)

In Ezekiel 34 we saw God's promise to personally shepherd his people through the Son of David. In Jeremiah 3:15, God promised to send his people shepherds after his own heart. And in 1 Peter 5, Peter echoes these passages. It's almost as if he has Ezekiel 34 open right in front of him as he charges pastors to shepherd God's flock as God would have them.

14. What do all these passages, taken together, teach about pastors' job description and about how pastors should minister to God's people?

15. What do these passages have to say to the person who is skeptical or uneasy about authority in the church? How do these passages confront, comfort, and encourage such an individual?

16. Can you give an example of a leader who you have witnessed shepherding others in ways that look something like the divine shepherd?

LESSON 3

Elders: Ministers of the Word and Shepherds of the Church

Audio link: *https://www.9marks.org/church-leadership-lesson-3/*

GETTING STARTED

1. What do churches typically expect their pastors to do? List everything you can think of.

2. Do you think there's anything churches expect pastors to do that they shouldn't or anything that churches don't expect but should?

MAIN IDEA

Elders are called to lead the church by teaching God's word, shepherding the flock one by one, and serving as examples of godly character.

DIGGING IN

In the New Testament, the church's spiritual leaders are interchangeably referred to as "elders," "overseers," and "pastors" (e.g., Acts 20:17, 28; Titus 1:5, 7). Since "elder" is the most common title, that's the one we'll use.

In this lesson, we're going to look at what elders are supposed to do. In the next lesson, we'll think about the qualifications for being an elder. And as we have in the previous lessons, we will examine our topic with an open Bible.

In 1 Peter 5, Peter directly addresses local church elders, saying,

> [1] I exhort the elders among you, as a fellow elder and a witness of the
> sufferings of Christ, as well as a partaker in the glory that is going to
> be revealed: [2] shepherd the flock of God that is among you, exercis-
> ing oversight, not under compulsion, but willingly, as God would
> have you; not for shameful gain, but eagerly; [3] not domineering over
> those in your charge, but being examples to the flock. [4] And when
> the chief Shepherd appears, you will receive the unfading crown
> of glory. [5] Likewise, you who are younger, be subject to the elders.
> Clothe yourselves, all of you, with humility toward one another, for
> "God opposes the proud but gives grace to the humble." (5:1–5)

1. On what basis does Peter appeal to the elders (v. 1)? Why do you think he mentions these things before exhorting the elders?

2. What is the main command Peter gives to the elders (v. 2)?

3. What does it mean, practically, to shepherd a church? What are some examples of shepherding?

4. In verses 2 and 3, Peter alternates between telling the elders how they should and shouldn't shepherd the flock. Fill in the chart below in order to map out what Peter is saying, and then answer the following questions.

Don't Shepherd Like This . . .	Instead, Shepherd Like *This* . . .

- What strikes you about what Peter says *not* to do? Why do you think he prohibits these things?

- Does anything strike you about what Peter says *to* do?

- What kind of fruit do you think would come from a ministry in which the elders faithfully obeyed Peter's instructions?

5. What does Peter say will happen to faithful elders when Jesus comes back (v. 4)? Why should this encourage elders? Why should it humble them?

6. What does Peter tell the rest of the church to do in response to the elders' ministry (v. 5)? Why does this require humility on our part?

In Acts 20, Paul gathers the elders of the church in Ephesus together as he passes through town on his way to Jerusalem in order to instruct them about how to carry out their ministry. We read,

> [17] Now from Miletus he sent to Ephesus and called the elders of the church to come to him. [18] And when they came to him, he said to them:
>
> "You yourselves know how I lived among you the whole time from the first day that I set foot in Asia, [19] serving the Lord with all humility and with tears and with trials that happened to me through the plots of the Jews; [20] how I did not shrink from declaring to you anything that was profitable, and teaching you in public and from house to house, [21] testifying both to Jews and to Greeks of repentance toward God and of faith in our Lord Jesus Christ. [22] And now, behold, I am going to Jerusalem, constrained by the Spirit, not knowing what will happen to me there, [23] except that the Holy Spirit testifies to me in every city that imprisonment and afflictions await me. [24] But I do not account my life of any value nor as precious to myself, if only I may finish my course and the ministry that I received from the Lord Jesus, to testify to the gospel of the grace of God. [25] And now, behold, I know that none of you among whom I have gone about proclaiming the kingdom will see my face again. [26] Therefore I testify to you this day that I am innocent of the blood of all, [27] for I did not shrink from declaring to you the whole counsel of God. [28] Pay careful attention to your-

selves and to all the flock, in which the Holy Spirit has made you
overseers, to care for the church of God, which he obtained with
his own blood. 29 I know that after my departure fierce wolves will
come in among you, not sparing the flock; 30 and from among your
own selves will arise men speaking twisted things, to draw away
the disciples after them. 31 Therefore be alert, remembering that
for three years I did not cease night or day to admonish everyone
with tears. 32 And now I commend you to God and to the word
of his grace, which is able to build you up and to give you the in-
heritance among all those who are sanctified. 33 I coveted no one's
silver or gold or apparel. 34 You yourselves know that these hands
ministered to my necessities and to those who were with me. 35 In
all things I have shown you that by working hard in this way we
must help the weak and remember the words of the Lord Jesus,
how he himself said, 'It is more blessed to give than to receive.'"

36 And when he had said these things, he knelt down and
prayed with them all. 37 And there was much weeping on the part
of all; they embraced Paul and kissed him, 38 being sorrowful
most of all because of the word he had spoken, that they would
not see his face again. And they accompanied him to the ship.

7. Why does Paul so extensively discuss his own way of life and teaching in this address to the Ephesian elders? What is he doing?

8. What aspects of ministry characterized Paul's way of life among the Ephesians (vv. 18–21, 27, 31, 33–35)?

9. How does Paul's life hold up to Peter's teaching about how elders should live and exercise their ministries? (Look for explicit points of comparison between the two; there are lots!)

10. What does Paul charge the Ephesian elders to do? List all of his directions for them (see esp. vv. 28, 31, 35).

11. Looking over these two passages, do you think elders have an easy job? Why or why not?

12. Hebrews 13:17 says, "Obey your leaders and submit to them, for they are keeping watch over your souls, as those who will have to give an account. Let them do this with joy and not with groaning, for that would be of no advantage to you." Given all that elders are responsible to do, what are some ways that you can help ensure that they shepherd you with joy and not with groaning?

13. What are some specific ways you can pray for your pastors or elders that are based on these passages? Write a few out and then discuss them. Will you commit to regularly praying these things for your elders?

LESSON 4

Finding the Right Men: Qualifications for Elders

Audio link: *https://www.9marks.org/church-leadership-lesson-4/*

GETTING STARTED

1. What kinds of things qualify people for leadership in business? What about in local communities? In the government?

2. What do you think qualifies someone for spiritual leadership in the church?

MAIN IDEA

Elders must be men of consistently exemplary Christian character, must lead their families well, and must be able to teach God's word.

DIGGING IN

In 1 Timothy 3:1–7, Paul lays out qualifications for elders. He writes,

> 1 The saying is trustworthy: If anyone aspires to the office of
> overseer, he desires a noble task. 2 Therefore an overseer must
> be above reproach, the husband of one wife, sober-minded,
> self-controlled, respectable, hospitable, able to teach, 3 not a
> drunkard, not violent but gentle, not quarrelsome, not a lover
> of money. 4 He must manage his own household well, with all
> dignity keeping his children submissive, 5 for if someone does
> not know how to manage his own household, how will he care
> for God's church? 6 He must not be a recent convert, or he may
> become puffed up with conceit and fall into the condemnation
> of the devil. 7 Moreover, he must be well thought of by outsiders,
> so that he may not fall into disgrace, into a snare of the devil.

Note: In this passage, Paul describes the office of elder using the term *episkopos*, which means "overseer." Throughout the New Testament, the terms "elder" and "overseer" refer to the same office. (See, for example, the nearly identical list of qualifications in Titus 1:5–9, as well as Acts 20:17, 28; Philippians 1:1; 1 Timothy 5:17–19; and 1 Peter 5:1–4.)

1. In this passage, Paul presents a series of qualifications for men who desire to be elders. List them.

2. What does it mean to be "above reproach" (v. 2)?

3. The Greek phrase translated "husband of one wife" could also be translated as "one-woman man" (v. 2). What does this qualification require of married men?

4. The words "sober-minded," "self-controlled," and "respectable" all refer to similar qualities (v. 2). List some concrete examples of what these might look like in action.

5. Why do you think hospitality is a qualification for an elder (v. 2)? What should Christian hospitality consist of?

New Testament scholar D. A. Carson has observed that perhaps the most extraordinary thing about the biblical qualifications for elders is that they are not all that extraordinary.[1] In fact, almost all of them are required of all Christians elsewhere in the New Testament (see Matt. 5:27–30; Rom. 12:13; Eph. 6:4; 1 Thess. 4:12; Titus 2:1–12; 1 Pet. 1:13). The only two qualifications that are not required of all Christians but are required of elders are to be mature in the faith and "able to teach" (1 Tim. 3:2).

6. Read Titus 1:9–10. Why is it important for elders to be able to teach (v. 2)?

7. Read 1 Timothy 2:11–15. If all elders are required to be able to teach and teaching the church is one of their main responsibilities (Titus 1:9–10), does Scripture allow women to be elders?

1 D. A Carson, "Defining Elders," 9Marks, January 4, 1999, https://www.9marks.org/.

8. What do the qualifications listed in verse 3 (not a drunkard, not violent but gentle, not quarrelsome, not a lover of money) have in common?

9. Why does Paul insist that a man must manage his household well in order to be an elder (vv. 4–5)?

10. Why could a recent convert be susceptible to becoming puffed up with conceit and falling into the condemnation of the devil (v. 6)?

11. In verse 7 Paul insists that an elder must be well-thought-of by outsiders. What is at stake in an elder's reputation among non-Christians?

12. In verses 6 and 7, Paul warns twice against elders falling into Satan's traps. In what ways are elders particularly susceptible to temptation?

13. How can this list of qualifications guide your prayers for your church's leaders? List specific examples.

14. What are some practical ways you can encourage these qualities in other church members? What are some ways you can cultivate these qualities yourself? Remember, elders are required to meet these standards in order to serve as examples for the whole church to imitate (see 1 Pet. 5:3).

LESSON 5

Deacons: Servants of the Church

Audio link: *https://www.9marks.org/church-leadership-lesson-5/*

GETTING STARTED

1. When practical needs arise in your church, who tends to take care of them?

2. What are some of the practical needs that arise in your church? What challenges can they pose to the unity of your church?

MAIN IDEA

Deacons are to serve the church by caring for its practical needs and freeing up the elders to devote themselves to the ministry of the word and prayer.

DIGGING IN

What we see in Acts 6:1–7 is probably the historical roots of the office of deacon. It begins with a tense conflict:

> 1 Now in these days when the disciples were increasing in number, a complaint by the Hellenists arose against the Hebrews because their widows were being neglected in the daily distribution. 2 And the twelve summoned the full number of the disciples and said, "It is not right that we should give up preaching the word of God to serve tables. 3 Therefore, brothers, pick out from among you seven men of good repute, full of the Spirit and of wisdom, whom we will appoint to this duty. 4 But we will devote ourselves to prayer and to the ministry of the word." 5 And what they said pleased the whole gathering, and they chose Stephen, a man full of faith and of the Holy Spirit, and Philip, and Prochorus, and Nicanor, and Timon, and Parmenas, and Nicolaus, a proselyte of Antioch. 6 These they set before the apostles, and they prayed and laid their hands on them. 7 And the word of God continued to increase, and the number of the disciples multiplied greatly in Jerusalem, and a great many of the priests became obedient to the faith. (6:1–7)

1. What problem did the church in Jerusalem face in this passage (v. 1)?

2. What was the apostles' solution to this problem (vv. 2–4)?

3. What kind of men did the apostles tell the congregation to pick out for this task (v. 3)?

4. Why did the apostles delegate this task (v. 4)?

The Greek word from which we get the term "deacon" is *diakonos*, which means servant. In the New Testament, this term was used to describe many different kinds of work, including waiting tables (the related verb is used in 6:2). And the apostles resolved to devote themselves to the *diakonia*, the ministry of the word and prayer (6:4). Thus, while Acts 6 doesn't use the term "deacon" to describe the men who handled the distribution of food, it seems probable that Luke recorded this incident to show the historical origins of what later became the office of deacon.

By the time the apostle Paul wrote 1 Timothy, the office of deacon was apparently well established in many churches (see Phil. 1:1). Thus, in 1 Timothy 3, after listing the qualifications for elders, Paul lays out the qualifications for deacons as well:

> 8 Deacons likewise must be dignified, not double-tongued, not addicted to much wine, not greedy for dishonest gain. 9 They must hold the mystery of the faith with a clear conscience. 10 And let them also be tested first; then let them serve as deacons if they prove themselves blameless. 11 Their wives [or "deaconesses"] likewise must be dignified, not slanderers, but sober-minded, faithful in all things. 12 Let deacons each be the husband of one wife, managing their children and their own households well. 13 For those who serve well as deacons gain a good standing for themselves and also great confidence in the faith that is in Christ Jesus. (3:8–13)

5. In verse 8, Paul lists several qualifications for deacons that pertain to a person's character. List these qualifications and then try to find a word or phrase that summarizes them. What overall picture do these qualifications paint?

6. What does it mean to "hold the mystery of the faith with a clear conscience" (v. 9)?

7. Why do you think Paul insists that deacons be tested before they serve (v. 10)? (For a similar line of thought, see Paul's instruction that an elder must not be a recent convert in verse 6.)

8. What does Paul require of deacons in terms of family life (v. 12)?

9. Read 1 Timothy 3:4–5. What is present in this qualification for elders that is absent in the qualification for deacons in 3:12? What do you think this teaches us about the difference between the two offices?

10. What do deacons who serve well gain (v. 13)? Why do you think this is?

11. Are there any qualifications for elders that aren't qualifications for deacons? What does that tell us about the difference between elders' and deacons' responsibilities?

At the beginning of this lesson, we argued that Acts 6 gives historical background to the office of deacon but does not describe the founding of the office itself (note that the term "deacon" isn't used in the passage). If that's the case, then the office of deacon is only mentioned two or perhaps three times in the New Testament (Phil. 1:1; 1 Tim. 3:8–13; possibly Rom. 16:1).

According to the little information that Scripture gives us, it seems that the role of deacons is to care for the church's practical needs in order to enable the elders to focus on the ministry of the word and prayer as the apostles did (Acts 6:4). That's why deacons are required to be people of godly character, integrity, and proven faith but are not required to be able to teach nor tasked with leading the church the way the elders are.

12. Within that basic framework, what are some more specific ways deacons should serve in the church? What are some needs in your church that deacons could address?

13. What are some challenges deacons face? What are some ways you can encourage and pray for your church's deacons in light of these challenges?

LESSON 6

Your Responsibility for the Church

Audio link: *https://www.9marks.org/church-leadership-lesson-6/*

GETTING STARTED

1. What are some things (or people!) in your life that you're responsible for?

2. How do those responsibilities affect your day-to-day life, priorities, and decisions?

MAIN IDEA

Elders have a special responsibility to preach the word, lead the church, and equip the saints for the work of the ministry. A congregation should submit to their leadership, guard the church's doctrine, and protect the church's membership.

DIGGING IN

The previous lessons of this study have demonstrated that elders are responsible for leading and teaching the church. And when they lead well, they don't monopolize the church's ministry but equip others to do ministry. In Ephesians 4 Paul writes,

> 11 And he gave the apostles, the prophets, the evangelists, the shep-
> herds and teachers, 12 to equip the saints for the work of ministry, for
> building up the body of Christ, 13 until we all attain to the unity of the
> faith and of the knowledge of the Son of God, to mature manhood,
> to the measure of the stature of the fullness of Christ, 14 so that we
> may no longer be children, tossed to and fro by the waves and car-
> ried about by every wind of doctrine, by human cunning, by craft-
> iness in deceitful schemes. 15 Rather, speaking the truth in love, we
> are to grow up in every way into him who is the head, into Christ,
> 16 from whom the whole body, joined and held together by every
> joint with which it is equipped, when each part is working properly,
> makes the body grow so that it builds itself up in love (4:11–16).

1. According to Ephesians 4, who does the ministry in the church and who equips the church to do ministry?

2. What does Ephesians 4 teach us about how elders should spend their time?

3. What happens to a church if the pastors spend all their time running ministries rather than equipping others to do ministry? What does Paul say will happen to a church where pastors focus on equipping the saints to do ministry?

Since pastors both lead and equip the church, the congregation has an obligation to follow their leadership and carry out the work of the ministry. First, a congregation must submit to its leaders. This is seen, for example, in Hebrews 13:17, which says, "Obey your leaders and submit to them, for they are keeping watch over your souls, as those who will have to give an account. Let them do this with joy and not with groaning, for that would be of no advantage to you."

4. What does it mean to "obey" and "submit" to leaders?

5. How can a congregation submit to their elders in a way that brings the elders joy?

Second, a congregation, equipped for ministry, must guard the church's doctrine. This is seen, for example, in Galatians 1, one of the most heated passages in all of Paul's letters. He writes,

> [1] Paul, an apostle—not from men nor through man, but through Jesus Christ and God the Father, who raised him from the dead—[2] and all the brothers who are with me,

To the churches of Galatia:

[3] Grace to you and peace from God our Father and the Lord
Jesus Christ, [4] who gave himself for our sins to deliver us from
the present evil age, according to the will of our God and Father,
[5] to whom be the glory forever and ever. Amen.

[6] I am astonished that you are so quickly deserting him who
called you in the grace of Christ and are turning to a different
gospel—[7] not that there is another one, but there are some who
trouble you and want to distort the gospel of Christ. [8] But even if
we or an angel from heaven should preach to you a gospel con-
trary to the one we preached to you, let him be accursed. [9] As we
have said before, so now I say again: If anyone is preaching to you
a gospel contrary to the one you received, let him be accursed.

[10] For am I now seeking the approval of man, or of God? Or
am I trying to please man? If I were still trying to please man,
I would not be a servant of Christ. (1:1–10)

6. What is Paul astonished about (vv. 6–7)?

7. What are those who are troubling the Galatians doing (v. 7)?

8. On whom does Paul pronounce a curse (twice!) in verses 8 and 9? Why is preaching a false gospel such a serious matter?

9. Who is Paul's letter addressed to? Is he only speaking to the church's leaders?

10. According to this passage, who is ultimately responsible for ensuring that the church is teaching sound doctrine?

Finally, a congregation must protect the purity of the church's membership. This is seen, for example, in 1 Corinthians 5, where Paul addresses another serious issue that arose in a local church—except this time the issue wasn't doctrinal, it was moral. Paul writes,

> [1]It is actually reported that there is sexual immorality among you,
> and of a kind that is not tolerated even among pagans, for a man
> has his father's wife. [2]And you are arrogant! Ought you not rather to
> mourn? Let him who has done this be removed from among you.
> [3]For though absent in body, I am present in spirit; and as if pres-
> ent, I have already pronounced judgment on the one who did such
> a thing. [4]When you are assembled in the name of the Lord Jesus
> and my spirit is present, with the power of our Lord Jesus, [5]you are
> to deliver this man to Satan for the destruction of the flesh, so that
> his spirit may be saved in the day of the Lord. (vv. 1–5)

11. What are the Corinthians tolerating (v. 1)? What is their attitude toward this person and his sin (v. 2)?

12. What does Paul tell the Corinthians to do about this (v. 2)?

13. When and how, specifically, does Paul tell the church to address this man's sin (vv. 3–5)?

14. Who does Paul hold to be finally accountable for tolerating this man's sin?

In these two passages we see that it is the local church as a whole who is ultimately responsible for ensuring that sound doctrine is preached and the lives of church members are in line with the gospel. This means that all of us have a responsibility for the church's teaching and its members' lives, and all of us will give an account to God for how we've handled this responsibility.

15. If you're accountable in some sense for the godly testimony of the members of your church, how should you respond when someone sins against you? Does it matter how serious the sin is? What about if you discover a serious sin in someone's life?

16. As we saw in Galatians 1, every church member is responsible for ensuring that their church preaches the gospel faithfully. What are some practical ways you can exercise this responsibility? Consider Acts 17:11 as a starting point.

FOR FURTHER STUDY

To learn more about the whole congregation's responsibility for its membership, discipline, and doctrine, study Matthew 18:15–17, 2 Corinthians 2:6, and 2 Timothy 4:3.

Teacher's Notes for Lesson 1

DIGGING IN

1. Christ is the "head" of the church (5:23).
2. As the church's "head," Christ is not only its source of life and salvation but also its highest and supreme authority. He is in charge, governing the church by his authoritative word.
3. The church recognizes and responds to Christ's headship by submitting to his authority (Eph. 5:24).
4. Scripture, though written by human authors, ultimately originates from God himself. He "breathed out" these words just as our words are breathed out of our mouths (2 Tim. 3:16). Since Scripture ultimately originates from God himself, it is not subject to any higher authority. It is instead the supreme authority on all issues it speaks to.
5. This phrase shows us that Scripture is sufficient to train God's people for life and godliness. It gives us everything we need to live our lives wholly devoted to God. Therefore, we need not look outside Scripture for instruction on how Christians should live or how the church should be ordered.

6. Since governing the church is a good work, we should trust that God has sufficiently revealed to us in his word everything we need to know about it.
7. Paul wants Timothy to organize the church according to the biblical principles (the "order") established by Scripture. The word "order" implies that Scripture provides us with a normative pattern that every church should conform itself to.
8. "Appoint elders in every town as I directed you."
9. Scripture teaches that there are two offices in the church: pastors (also called elders) and deacons.
10. Pastors lead the church by giving themselves to the ministry of the word (teaching) and prayer. Deacons serve the church by meeting the tangible needs of the congregation.
11. Answers will vary.
12. Answers will vary. Essentially, a church that doesn't follow biblical instructions is leaning on its own wisdom, failing to honor God, failing to teach Christians how to live the Christian life, and probably not caring for its members in the way that Scripture commands.
13. Answers will vary.

Teacher's Notes for Lesson 2

DIGGING IN

1. Nebuchadnezzar says that God does whatever he pleases among the inhabitants of his earth and no one can hinder his plans or question his justice. In other words, God exercises complete sovereignty and authority over human beings.

2. Answers will vary. Our hearts should rejoice, be humbled, and offer worship when we contemplate God's unrivaled sovereignty over everything. Too often pride wells up within us and we think, "That's not fair!" But to rebel in our hearts against God's rule is the very essence of sin. So we must cultivate appropriate reverence, awe, and humility before God, rejoicing that he is the king of all and we are his subjects.

3. Being made in God's image means (among other things) that humanity was created to exercise dominion over creation, righteously stewarding its resources and mirroring God's rule over it (Gen. 1:26, 28). Thus, in Genesis 1:28 God tells the first man and woman to be fruitful and multiply, to fill the earth and subdue it.

4. From this passage we learn that God has delegated a measure of authority over creation to all human beings. Further, we learn

that exercising authority over creation is part of what it means to be human. Since all of us are made in the image of God, all of us are to righteously exercise authority in specific ways.

5. According to David, when someone rules righteously over men, the effect is like the sun shining ever more brightly until it reaches full noon and like rain that waters the earth. This imagery shows that godly authority brings life, vitality, and growth to those who are under it. Personal experiences of this will vary, but hopefully participants will be able to recall positive experiences of authority figures like parents, teachers, church leaders, or government officials exercising authority in a righteous way.

6. An appropriate response would be something like, "Of course authority can be abused, and when it is, that's an awful thing. God clearly condemns that in his word. But the right use of authority reflects the character of God himself. He is Lord and he rules over all the universe. And he created us in his image, telling us to exercise authority over creation. Further, he gives specific kinds of authority to the government, parents, employers, and church leaders. This authority is meant to bless, protect, help, and build up others and is to be exercised in the fear of God and in submission to his will."

7. According to this passage, the shepherds of Israel have fed and clothed themselves while neglecting the sheep (vv. 2–3). Verse 4 tells us that they haven't strengthened the weak, healed the sick, bound up the injured, brought back the strayed, or sought out the lost. In other words, they've made themselves wealthy by exploiting the poor among Israel rather than bringing justice. Further, by living unrighteously, they've abdicated their

spiritual responsibility to lead the people in obeying God. The concrete events this passage refers to are probably the acts of economic exploitation that the leaders of Israel perpetrated against the nation.

8. As a result of the shepherds' unrighteousness and negligence, God's people are scattered over the face of the earth, becoming food for the wild beasts (vv. 5–6). This passage is referring to the exile, wherein, as an act of judgment for the people's—and especially the leaders'—sin, Israel was taken captive by a foreign nation.

9. In verses 11–16, God promises to:

   - Search for his sheep after they were scattered (vv. 11–12)
   - Bring them back into their own land (v. 13)
   - Feed them with good pasture (vv. 13–14)
   - Cause them to lie down in safety (v. 14)
   - Shepherd them himself (v. 15)
   - Seek the lost (v. 16)
   - Bring back those who strayed (v. 16)
   - Bind up the injured (v. 16)
   - Strengthen the weak (v. 16)
   - Destroy the fat and strong who have oppressed the flock (v. 16)

   In other words, God promises to personally care for his people, undoing the harm that the unrighteous shepherds brought and restoring his people's holistic well-being.

10. God's promise to gather and feed his sheep (vv. 11–14) reveals that he is a God who provides for his people and cares for all of their needs. His promise to seek the lost, bring back the strayed, and strengthen the weak (v. 16) reveals that he is compassionate and tender. He pities his people's weaknesses and personally condescends to care for them. His promise to destroy those who abused his people and to shepherd his people in justice (v. 16) reveals that he is holy and just. He will punish those who harm, exploit, and abuse others, and his rule over his people is perfectly righteous toward all.
11. God promises that after he rescues his flock, he will set up his servant David over them to shepherd them.
12. God fulfills this promise by sending Jesus, the Son of David and the good shepherd, to reign over his people and lead them in righteousness forever.
13. The prophecy of Jeremiah 3:15, that God will establish shepherds after his own heart, creates expectations that he will lead his people not just by his one chief shepherd (cf. 1 Pet. 5:4) but also by many other righteous shepherds under his authority. This prophecy is fulfilled in the church through Christ's gift of pastors (Eph. 4:8–12) who lead, teach God's word (Jer. 3:15), and shepherd according to God's will (1 Pet. 5:3).
14. All of these passages, taken together, teach us that pastors are to:
    - Lead the church righteously, imitating God's character (Jer. 3:15)
    - Feed God's people what they need, which is God's word (Jer. 3:15; John 21:15–17; 2 Tim. 4:2)

- Not exploit God's people for selfish gain but instead be examples of godliness (Ezek. 34:1–6; 1 Pet. 5:2)
- Give special care to members of the flock who are weak or ill (Ezek. 34:16; James 5:14), especially those who are spiritually weak or ill
- Pursue those who wander from the flock (Ezek. 34:16), exercising loving discipline that mirrors the way God handles us when we stray

15. Answers will vary. In short, by giving us a rich picture of the character of God and the way he exercises authority, these passages show us what God expects from those he has given earthly authority to. And what he expects is nothing less than shepherding the way he does. This means that abuse of authority is never God's will, and those who claim divine sanction for abusing authority are only showing that they don't deserve to wield that authority in the first place. This should comfort and encourage those who are skeptical of authority—and should undermine that skepticism!—because the authority God wants to see is an authority that reflects his own character, an authority that is righteous, compassionate, loving, and self-sacrificing for the good of others.
16. Answers will vary.

Teacher's Notes for Lesson 3

DIGGING IN

1. In verse 1, Peter appeals to the elders on the basis of (1) his status as a fellow elder, (2) his role as a witness of the sufferings of Christ, and (3) his share in the glory that is to come (which these elders also have). Peter probably mentions these things in order to remind the elders of his authority (as an eyewitness of Christ), his sympathy with their struggles (as a fellow elder), and of the hope of an eternal reward that awaits those who faithfully serve Christ.
2. The main command Peter gives to the elders is to shepherd the flock of God. Everything that follows describes how they must (or must not!) do this.
3. Practically speaking, to shepherd a church means
    - faithfully teaching the church God's word (John 21:15–17)
    - protecting the church from false teachers through careful teaching and discipline
    - leading the church as a whole in ways that are faithful to God's word

- attending to each church member's soul, caring for spiritual needs, helping to bear burdens, and leading each member to greater conformity to Christ

4. The completed chart should look something like this:

Don't Shepherd Like This....	Instead, Shepherd Like *This* ...
As though under compulsion (v. 2)	Exercise oversight (v. 2)
For shameful (i.e., selfish monetary) gain (v. 2)	Willingly (v. 2)
Domineering over those in your charge (v. 3)	As God would have you (v. 2)
	Eagerly (v. 2)
	Being examples to the flock (v.3)

Answers to the discussion questions will vary.

5. Peter says that when Jesus comes back, faithful elders will receive the unfading crown of glory (v. 4). This should encourage elders because through all the hardships they endure for Christ's sake now, they look forward to the enjoyment of an eternal reward. This should humble them because God's reward of their labors is a gracious gift they do not deserve. Further, Peter refers to Christ as the chief shepherd, which reminds the elders that they are undershepherds who are accountable to their Lord.

6. Peter tells the rest of the church to submit to the elders. This requires humility because submitting means being willing to follow and obey someone else's leadership and teaching and none of us, by nature, like to do that.

7. Paul extensively discusses his own way of life and teaching in this address to the Ephesian elders because he is holding himself up as an example for them to follow. In his personal conduct, his teaching, and his pastoral work, Paul established himself as a model. Now, when he has one last chance to speak to them, he is reminding them of this example so that they will follow it in their own ministries.

8. Paul's way of life among the Ephesians was characterized by:
    - serving the Lord with all humility and with tears (v. 19)
    - declaring to them everything that was profitable (v. 20), teaching in public and in people's homes (v. 20)
    - testifying to Jews and Greeks that they should repent and believe in Christ (v. 21)
    - declaring the whole counsel of God (v. 27)
    - day and night admonishing everyone with tears (v. 31)
    - not coveting anyone's possessions (v. 33)
    - working to support himself and provide for others so that he might be an example of Jesus's teaching that it is more blessed to give than to receive (vv. 34–35)

9. Paul's life is a vivid fulfillment and example of the things Peter says should characterize elders. As an apostle and church planter, Paul established the model that the elders in Ephesus were to follow by
    - setting an example of godliness for all the Christians to follow (1 Pet. 5:3)
    - diligently shepherding the flock at Ephesus (1 Pet. 5:2)

- doing so willingly, not under compulsion, and clearly not for selfish gain, since he coveted no one's money (1 Pet. 5:2–3)
- not domineering over those under his charge (1 Pet 5:3) but instead lovingly teaching, caring for, and exhorting them

10. Paul charges the Ephesian elders to:

    - pay careful attention to themselves and to all the flock (v. 28)
    - care for (literally "shepherd") the flock (v. 28)
    - protect against false teachers (v. 31)
    - help the weak (v. 35)

    By implication, Paul also exhorts the elders to follow everything he did in his ministry, namely, proclaiming the whole counsel of God, calling people to repent and believe, and personally ministering the gospel to everyone in their charge.

11. Answers will vary. Hopefully, people will recognize that serving as an elder is a difficult and demanding task since elders are required to faithfully teach, shepherd, protect against false teachers, and set an example of godliness for the whole church.
12. Answers will vary.
13. Answers will vary.

Teacher's Notes for Lesson 4

DIGGING IN

1. According to this passage, an elder must be:
   a. above reproach (v. 2)
   b. the husband of one wife (v. 2)
   c. sober minded (v. 2)
   d. self-controlled (v. 2)
   e. respectable (v. 2)
   f. hospitable (v. 2)
   g. able to teach (v. 2)
   h. not a drunkard (v. 3)
   i. not violent but gentle (v. 3)
   j. not quarrelsome (v. 3)
   k. not a lover of money (v. 3)
   l. a good manager of his household, keeping his children submissive (vv. 4–5)
   m. not a recent convert (v. 6)
   n. well thought of by outsiders (v. 7)

2. To be "above reproach" (v. 2) is to have a consistently godly character that is not open to the charge of living in any serious, overt sin. Being "above reproach" doesn't mean being perfect. All Christians still struggle with sin (James 3:1–2). But in order to be an elder, a man must exhibit consistent and thorough godliness.

3. This qualification means that a married man must be completely faithful to his wife. It doesn't seem that this verse requires that a man be married (after all, Paul commends singleness for the purpose of ministry in 1 Corinthians 7). Rather, since the vast majority of men marry, this verse simply assumes that and asserts that an elder must be sexually faithful. Obviously, a single man who would be an elder must have sexual integrity as well.

4. Answers will vary.

5. Hospitality is a qualification for being an elder because elders must generously care for others (v. 2). Christian hospitality should consist of welcoming fellow Christians into one's home, especially Christians who are in need, providing for fellow Christians' material needs, and encouraging them spiritually.

6. According to Titus 1:9–10, it is important for elders to be able to teach because they must instruct the church in truth and refute those who teach false doctrine.

7. In 1 Timothy 2:12, Paul writes, "I do not permit a woman to teach or to exercise authority over a man." And he grounds this command not in a cultural custom or temporary circumstance but in creation itself, indicating that this is a normative, ongoing command for all churches. Since authoritative teach-

ing is a key responsibility of elders, this means that Scripture does not permit women to serve as elders. Rather, only qualified men should fill that role.

8. The qualifications listed in verse 3 all refer to self-control or mastery of one's appetites. A man who isn't a drunkard controls his use of alcohol. A man who is not violent controls his desire for revenge and humbles himself to serve someone else in love. And a man who is not a lover of money has mastered the desire for material things and thus treats money and possessions as gifts from God entrusted to him so that he would use them faithfully rather than coveting them and hoarding them.

9. Paul insists that a man must manage his household well in order to be an elder (vv. 4–5) because a man's home life is one of the truest tests of his character. A man lives with his wife and children. And he is responsible before God to lead them spiritually. Whether a man's children obey him is a test of how well he teaches them, disciplines them, and models godly living for them. Thus, whether a man is a godly leader will be evident in his home life. That's why Paul asks, "If someone does not know how to manage his own household, how will he care for God's church?" (v. 5).

10. A recent convert could be susceptible to becoming puffed up with conceit and falling into the condemnation of the devil (v. 6) because he has not developed the kind of tested character that comes from faithfully following Jesus over a long time. If a new convert is put in a position of prominence as an elder, it is possible that he will let the privilege go to his head. He may begin to think of himself more highly than he ought. And, as Scripture teaches, pride goes before a fall. Thus, an

elder must be someone whose character and maturity have been tested and proved through a relatively long course of following Christ.

11. What's at stake in an elder's reputation among non-Christians is the reputation of Christ in the world. All Christians are called to represent Christ to the world and to commend the gospel by their good deeds. All Christians bear the name of Christ. Yet, elders—as the officially recognized leaders of the church—have a special responsibility to represent Christ to the world and a heightened visibility before the world. The world will look first to the church's leaders to see if they live according to what they teach. If a church's leaders are hypocrites, they discredit the gospel and the church in the eyes of the world.

12. As we discussed in question 10, elders are particularly susceptible to temptation because they are in a position of prominence. This can easily lead to pride and arrogance. Elders can also be tempted to wield their influence harshly (1 Pet. 5:3) or for their own selfish gain (1 Pet. 5:2). And there are many more ways that elders can be tempted.

13. Answers will vary.

14. Answers will vary.

Teacher's Notes for Lesson 5

DIGGING IN

1. The problem the church in Jerusalem faced in this passage was that Hellenistic (Greek-speaking) members of the congregation were complaining against the Hebrew church members because the Greek widows were being overlooked in the daily distribution of food (v. 1).
2. The apostles' solution to this problem was to have the congregation select seven wise and godly men whom the apostles would appoint to take care of the daily distribution of food (vv. 2–4).
3. The apostles told the congregation to pick out men who were of good repute and full of the Holy Spirit and wisdom (v. 3).
4. The apostles delegated this task because they had to devote themselves to the ministry of the word and prayer and it would have been wrong for them to neglect that ministry in order to attend to the distribution of food (v. 4).
5. The qualifications for deacons in Paul's list that pertain to a person's character are:
    - dignified
    - not double-tongued

- not addicted to much wine
- not greedy for dishonest gain

One word that summarizes all of these is "self-control." Another is "integrity." A deacon must be admirable in his conduct, have control of his appetites, and speak truthfully.

6. To "hold the mystery of the faith with a clear conscience" means to be sound in both belief and action. To hold the mystery of the faith is to steadfastly believe the good news that God has revealed in Christ. And to do so with a clear conscience means living in a way that does not undermine one's claim to follow Christ (1 Tim. 3:9).

7. Paul insists that deacons be tested before they serve because they are given significant responsibility (v. 10). In order to address the church's physical needs, they will be entrusted with material resources, and they will interact with many different members of the church. Thus, they must demonstrate that they are able to handle such a responsibility with integrity and diligence before being entrusted with it.

8. In terms of their family life, Paul requires that deacons be faithful to their wives and manage their households well (v. 12).

9. In Paul's qualifications for elders (but not for deacons), he reasons, "If someone does not know how to manage his own household, how will he care for God's church?" This teaches us that Paul expected elders to care for the church—that is, to lead it—in a similar way to how a husband leads and cares for his family. Paul not including this argument when discussing deacons seems to indicate that deacons do not have the kind of authoritative leadership role that elders do.

10. Deacons who serve well gain "a good standing for themselves and also great confidence in the faith that is in Christ Jesus" (1 Tim. 3:13). This is because faithfully serving God and his people results in being commended in God's sight and before the church. Further, faithfully serving God and his people builds up one's confidence in Christ and in the power of the gospel to transform one into his image.
11. The one qualification for elders that isn't a qualification for deacons is that elders must be able to teach (1 Tim. 3:2). This tells us that one of the responsibilities of the office of elder is to teach God's word. On the other hand, it is not one of the responsibilities of the office of deacon. That doesn't mean that deacons can't teach the Bible. It simply means that it is not one of their responsibilities as deacons. Thus, just as deacons are not charged with overseeing the church as elders are, neither are they required to teach the word as elders are.
12. Answers will vary.
13. Answers will vary.

Teacher's Notes for Lesson 6

DIGGING IN

1. Elders ("shepherds and teachers") equip the saints to do the work of the ministry. In other words, elders are the supply line and members the front line of ministry in the church.
2. Elders need to give the bulk of their time to the ministry of teaching, which equips the saints to care for one another and evangelize the lost.
3. Regarding the first question, answers will vary. Essentially, a church where the pastors are doing all the ministry is a church where the congregation isn't embracing its responsibility to love, care for, and spiritually nurture one another. In these situations pastors often burn out and the church won't be well cared for since a pastor (or even a group of pastors) can't care for every need in the church. According to Paul, when pastors focus on equipping and members embrace their responsibility to do the work of ministry, the church is built up and nurtured into maturity. The body "builds itself up in love" (4:16).
4. Insofar as the elders are not leading the church away from the gospel, a congregation should heed their teaching, trust their judgments, and follow their leadership.

5. Answers will vary. A congregation can submit to their elders in a way that brings them joy primarily by embracing a posture of trust toward the elders and handling conflict or disagreement in a biblical manner that doesn't foster division.
6. Paul was astonished that the Galatians were deserting the God who called them in the grace of Christ and instead turning to a different gospel, which was really no gospel at all (vv. 6–7).
7. Those who are troubling the Galatians are distorting the gospel of Christ (v. 7).
8. In verses 8 and 9, Paul twice pronounces a curse on anyone who preaches a "gospel" other than the true gospel. Preaching a false gospel is such a serious matter because all of our eternal destinies hang on our belief in the gospel.
9. Paul's letter is addressed to the churches of Galatia (v. 1). He's not just speaking to the churches' leaders; he's speaking to everyone in those churches!
10. According to this passage, all the members of local churches are ultimately responsible for ensuring that the church is teaching sound doctrine.
11. The Corinthians are tolerating a church member who is having a sexual relationship with his father's wife (v. 1). Their attitude toward this person and his sin is one of arrogant boasting and approval (v. 2).
12. Paul tells the Corinthians to remove this man from their fellowship (v. 2).

13. Specifically, Paul tells them to remove this man from their fellowship when they come together as a church. When they are all assembled together, they must remove him from their membership, which is what Paul is getting at when he speaks of delivering the man to Satan (vv. 3–5).

14. In this passage Paul rebukes the whole church for tolerating this man's sin. Further, he tells the whole church to act in order to remove the man from fellowship. Thus, Paul holds the whole church, not just its leaders, accountable for this moral issue.

15. Since we are in some sense accountable for the godly testimony of the members of our church, we should carefully consider what we need to do when someone sins against us. If it's something minor, we should probably just pass over it, forgive them, and move on (Prov. 19:11; 1 Pet. 4:8). If the sin is more serious, we should confront them according to Jesus's instructions in Matthew 18:15–17. If the person doesn't respond to our private rebuke, then, in obedience to Jesus's teachings, we should involve others in the church. If you come to learn about a serious sin in someone else's life, you have a responsibility to do something about it. If you know the person well, it may be wise to privately confront him or her. If you don't know the person well, you may want to talk to one of your church's elders about it. Be wary of the temptation to gossip, but know that asking a church leader to help address a serious sin in someone's life is not gossip. It's seeking to turn a sinner from the error of his or her way in order to save that person from death and cover over a multitude of sins (James 5:19–20).

16. Here are some ways you could faithfully exercise your responsibility to ensure that your church's preaching is faithful to the gospel:

    - Regularly pray for your pastor and others who teach in your church. Pray that all of their teaching would be faithful to God's word.
    - Study Scripture on your own so that you will be better able to discern error when it comes across your path.
    - Pray that God would give you a humble, gracious spirit and the courage to confront error when that may be necessary.
    - If you hear something from a teacher in your church that seems wrong, ask a trusted, mature Christian who knows the Bible well for his or her opinion, or ask the teacher for clarification. Assume that he is in the right and that you simply misunderstood. Patiently listen to his explanation. And if you become convinced that your teacher has taught an error, approach another leader in the church to let him know your concern.

IX 9Marks

Building Healthy Churches

9Marks exists to equip church leaders with a biblical vision and practical resources for displaying God's glory to the nations through healthy churches.

To that end, we want to see churches characterized by these nine marks of health:

1. Expositional Preaching
2. Gospel Doctrine
3. A Biblical Understanding of Conversion and Evangelism
4. Biblical Church Membership
5. Biblical Church Discipline
6. A Biblical Concern for Discipleship and Growth
7. Biblical Church Leadership
8. A Biblical Understanding of the Practice of Prayer
9. A Biblical Understanding and Practice of Missions

Find all our Crossway titles and other resources at 9Marks.org.